Rodeo Cowboy

Phil Kettle
illustrated by Craig Smith

Distributed in
the United States of America
by Pacific Learning
P.O. Box 2723
Huntington Beach, CA
92647-0723

Website:
www.pacificlearning.com

Published by Black Hills
(an imprint of Toocool Rules
Pty Ltd)
PO Box 2073
Fitzroy MDC VIC 3065
Australia
61+3+9419-9406

First published in the United States by Black Hills in 2004.
American editorial by Pacific Learning in 2004.
Text copyright © Phillip Kettle, 2003.
Illustration copyright © Toocool Rules Pty Limited, 2003.

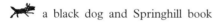 a black dog and Springhill book

Printed in China through Colorcraft Ltd, Hong Kong

ISBN 1 920924 16 7
PL-6216

10 9 8 7 6 5 4 3 2 1   08 07 06 05 04

Contents

Uncle Buck

Dog

Roberto

Toocool's mom

Toocool

Chapter 1
Toocool Ranch

Uncle Buck was coming to the Toocool Ranch for the weekend.

Roberto was also spending the night. He'd heard about Uncle Buck. Uncle Buck was the greatest. He lived on a cattle ranch out west.

When Uncle Buck arrived, he shook my hand.

"Howdy, pardner," he said. He squashed my hand like it was made of jelly. It's a good thing I'm so strong. Roberto put his hands in his pockets.

Uncle Buck stood as tall as a tree. His shoulders hardly fit through the doorway. His hands were as rough as sandpaper. Uncle Buck was a real cowboy. You could tell by the way he talked.

"Toocool, have you been standing in a bucket of manure?" said Uncle Buck. "You've grown."

Do people smell bad as they get older?

"This is Roberto," I said.

"Howdy, Roberto," said Uncle Buck. He slapped Roberto on the back. Roberto nearly ended up in the next state.

"What are we doing this weekend?" I asked. Uncle Buck always had good ideas.

"Boys," he said, "this weekend you're in for a treat. I'm going to teach you how to be cowboys."

Chapter 2
Howdy, Cowboy

At Toocool Ranch, Bert the Rooster was our alarm clock. Roberto and I got up early and washed in the horse trough—just like the cowboys on TV.

After breakfast, we had our
first cowboy lesson in the
backyard. Uncle Buck got out
his whip and snapped it in the
air. It made an explosive
cracking sound.

"Wow," said Roberto.

"Now you try," said
Uncle Buck.

Roberto and I took turns with the whip until we knocked over Mom's potted plants.

"Buck, how many times have I told you about that whip?" Mom was the boss of this ranch.

7

Uncle Buck took the whip back. He gave Roberto and me each a rope. The end of the rope was tied into a large loop.

"What's this?" asked Roberto.

"A lasso," said Uncle Buck. He twirled the rope around his head. He threw the rope at some fence posts.

I twirled the rope around
my head. I was a natural. I was
Cowboy Toocool. I'd taken to
cowboy life like a fly to a
cow pie.

"You boys need to practice
to get the feel for it. I'll check
on you later," said Uncle Buck.

9

Roberto and I practiced for hours. Finally, I left Roberto to the fence posts. I was ready for the real thing.

In the back corral of the Toocool Ranch was a bull—a wild bull. Now I was ready for him.

Chapter 3
Lasso **Power**

Roberto rushed after me as I eyed the bull.

"Don't do it, Toocool. He'll rip you to pieces."

"There isn't a bull on this planet that could scare me," I said. I threw the lasso into the air. I twirled it. The bull pawed the ground.

"You're wearing red,"
shouted Roberto.
"That'll just
make him wild."

"Maybe it will," I said,
twirling the lasso, "and maybe it
won't." I threw the lasso. The
bull ducked his head. He
lowered his horns.

"Look out!" shouted
Roberto.

I twirled the lasso again.
It flew into the air. It landed
neatly over the bull's head.

The bull snorted. He tried
to duck out of the lasso. He
tried to spear me with his
horns. I hung on. We both
crashed to the ground.

Uncle Buck was back to check out our lasso work.

"You've caught yourself a mean one there," he said.

The bull lay down on the ground. Obviously he had fainted from the terror of facing Cowboy Toocool.

"Toocool, it's one thing to bring down a bull," said Uncle Buck, "but have you ever ridden one?"

I shook my head.

"Time for the Toocool Ranch Rodeo Championship," said Uncle Buck. "There's a prize for the winner."

"Yee-ha!" shouted Roberto. I didn't know why he was so happy. I was going to win that prize.

Chapter 4
Bucking Broncos

After lunch, I changed into my rodeo gear.

"Gee, Roberto. I reckon I could get a part in a cowboy movie," I said.

"Toocool, the only part you could get is in a horror movie. You could play the monster."

I ignored him. Roberto must be worried about riding a bucking bull. A quick look in the mirror proved I was the best-looking cowboy ever.

The farmhands had come to watch the show. They sat on the corral and cheered when they saw us.

Uncle Buck led a large bull
into the chute. It was the
meanest, wildest bull I'd ever
seen. Roberto won the toss and
chose to ride first.

"You've gotta ride him for
eight seconds to make it count,"
said Uncle Buck.

Roberto nodded.

The bull snorted, kicking and bucking. Roberto held on with all his might. The bull twirled. Roberto held on. Finally, the bull bucked extra hard and Roberto flew off his back.

The farmhands cheered as Roberto hit the ground. Roberto got up and rubbed his bruises.

"Toocool, I think I won the Rodeo Championship with that ride," said Roberto.

I'd see about that.

My bull was really mad.
I had trouble just getting on
his back.

The farmhands fell silent.
They knew they were about to
see the greatest rodeo rider in
the world. I gave the nod.

Chapter 5
Sitting Tight

Instead of bouncing and bucking, the bull stood still in the middle of the pen. How could I win the Rodeo Championship if the bull wouldn't move?

Dog came to my rescue. He raced into the pen and barked at the bull.

The bull began to buck. He was doing his best to throw me off. Good thing I am so strong. I needed to stay on for another three seconds.

The farmhands were cheering, "Toocool, Toocool, you're the greatest!"

I was concentrating so hard I almost didn't hear them.

Uncle Buck yelled, "Time's up!"

The bull must have heard
him. He gave a mighty final
buck. I went straight over his
head. Splash. I landed in the
horse trough.

"Well, now, Toocool and Roberto—you're both officially honest-to-goodness cowboys," said Uncle Buck.

"So who won the contest?" asked Roberto.

Uncle Buck thought it was a tie.

"There's no championship
winner this ride," he said. "I'll
just have to take both you
cowboys out for ice cream." He
winked at me.

I knew that wink meant that
I was really the best.

26

In my diary that night I wrote, *Toocool won the Rodeo Championship today, and his best friend, Roberto, came in a close second.*

I was getting pretty famous. There was probably no one on Earth who didn't know me by now. You'd have to be an alien from outer space not to have heard of the famous Toocool.

The End!

Toocool's
Rodeo Glossary

Chute—A small fenced area where bulls wait to be released into the main ring.

Farmhand—A hired farmworker.

Lasso—A rope with a loop at one end that tightens when pulled.

Rodeo—An event where cowboys show their skills.

Trough—A long, low bin that holds animal food or water.

Toocool's Map
The Ranch

chland

ree

Ranch

Hayshed
and
Stable

Good Pasture

omestead

Toocool's Quick Summary
Bull Riding

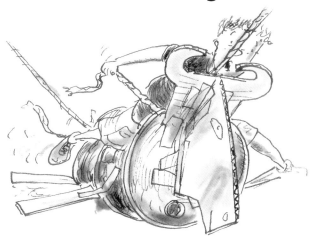

To be a bull rider, you need to be brave. Luckily for me, I am the bravest person that I know. Courage, strength, and great balance are some of the things that will help keep you on the bull. To become a great bull rider like I am, you should know a few words that we cowboys use.

Blow-up—A bull that runs a long way from the chute (where it enters the ring) before he bucks.

Bufford—A bull that is easy to ride, like the bull that Roberto rode.

Crow Hopper—A bull that doesn't buck, but jumps stiff-legged.

Honker—A really mean and powerful bull, like the one that I rode in the Championship.

Kissing the bull—When the cowboy's head hits the back of the bull's head.

Out the back door—When the rider is thrown over the back of the bull.

Now that you know all of these interesting terms, you can become a great cowboy, too.

The **Rodeo Bull**

Chuck Roast

Hamburgers

The Raging Bull

Brisket

Q & A with **Toocool**
He Answers His Own Questions

 **How long have you been interested in being a cowboy?**

Since forever. My Uncle Buck lives on a cattle ranch, and I've stayed there for vacations. Being a cowboy is cool. You get to wear cowboy boots, a big hat, and you don't ever have to take a shower. You also get to eat baked beans... a lot of them.

What's your favorite thing about being a cowboy?

Riding a bull. Throwing a lasso is fun, too. Cracking a whip makes a lot of noise, but it gives my mom a headache. Riding a bull would have to be the best thing.

 What do you like about rodeo riding?

Bulls are pretty big animals—huge. They're heavy, and they have horns. This is all dangerous stuff. It gives me a chance to show everyone my courage and great strength.

 Have you ever been scared while riding a bull?

No.

What is your least favorite kind of bull?

Well, I don't really like Dinks. Dinks don't buck very well. I think Hat Benders are my least favorite. A Hat Bender is a bull that doesn't buck. It just runs around the ring. You may as well be on a merry-go-round.

What could be worse than being "out the back door"?

If you've been thrown out the back door by a bull, you better hope that bull isn't a Slinger. A Slinger is a bull that tries to hit you with its head after it's thrown you off. No Slinger would dare take me on, but normal bull riders aren't that lucky.

38

What kind of people become rodeo riders?

You have to be very brave. Some riders start out brave, but lose their nerve after a bad ride. Uncle Buck lost his two front teeth "kissing the bull." It took him ages to get back on a bull. Of course, I'm a natural rodeo rider. I can't imagine ever losing my nerve.

Rodeo Quiz

How Much Do You Know about Bull Riding?

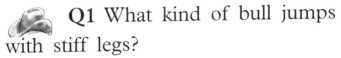 **Q1** What kind of bull jumps with stiff legs?

A. A bull without knees.

B. A Crow Hopper.

C. A bull on a pogo stick.

Q2 What does the term "out the back door" mean?

A. When you ask a bull to leave your house. *B.* When the rider is thrown over the back of the bull.

C. A noise made by a rude person.

Q3 What is a lasso?

A. A famous movie dog.

B. A rope with a loop at one end. **C.** A girl.

 Q4 What kind of bull is a Dink?

A. A bull that does not buck very well. **B.** A very small bull.

C. A bull with a strange name.

 Q5 Name Toocool's uncle.

A. Uncle Bick. **B.** Uncle Buck.

C. Aunt Mary.

 Q6 Who would ride a Hat Bender?

A. Toocool. **B.** Marcy.

C. Bert the Rooster.

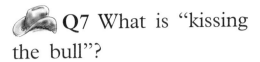**Q7** What is "kissing the bull"?

A. When you kiss a bull.

B. Flattering a rodeo clown.

C. When the cowboy's head hits the back of the bull's head.

Q8 Uncle Buck's hands are as rough as:

A. Sandpaper. **B.** Jelly. **C.** Manure.

Q9 To be a bull rider you need to be:

A. Brave. **B.** Scared. **C.** Funny.

Q10 Who is the alarm clock at Toocool Ranch?

A. Dog. **B.** Roberto. **C.** Bert the Rooster.

ANSWERS

🤠 *1* B. 🤠 *2* B. 🤠 *3* B.

🤠 *4* A. 🤠 *5* B. 🤠 *6* B.

🤠 *7* C. 🤠 *8* A. 🤠 *9* A.

🤠 *10* C.

If you got ten questions right, one day you could be a rodeo rider like Toocool. If you got more than five right, you might want to start by patting a bull. If you got fewer than five right, stick to the merry-go-round.

Space Captain

Earth is being invaded by aliens. Only one person can save the day—space captain **Toocool**.

Titles in the Toocool series